PIONEER TEXAS BUILDINGS

A Geometry Lesson

PIONEER TEXAS BUILDINGS

A Geometry Lesson

BY CLOVIS HEIMSATH

photographs by Maryann Heimsath
foreword by Louis Kahn

UNIVERSITY OF TEXAS PRESS, AUSTIN & LONDON

Type set by Southwestern Typographics Inc., Dallas
Printed by The Steck Company, Austin
Bound by Universal Bookbindery, Inc., San Antonio

ACKNOWLEDGMENTS

The author wishes to acknowledge the people and organizations that made this book possible. A summer study grant from Rice University was important in getting the project started. Encouragement and financial help from Miss Nina Cullinan were essential in continuing it.

The Texas Historical Society and local society members, particularly in Fredericksburg and Comfort, were of great help to the author, as were Miss Ima Hogg, Mrs. Hazel Ledbetter of Round Top, Diana and Bill Hobby of Houston, and Mrs. Nancy Negly of San Antonio.

Harrison Allen made an important contribution as graphic design consultant and Vilhelm Wolfhagen expertly processed the photographs.

Above all, the author acknowledges the many hundreds of homeowners throughout the Hill Country who have restored their early Texas homes and who encouraged the author and his wife in documenting them.

To Nina Cullinan, whose interest and encouragement made this book possible.

FOREWORD

To see these modest structures and see them again in the mind invokes wonder in what inspires the works of man. If I were asked what I now would choose to be, I would say "to be the creator of the new fairy tales." It is from the sense of the incredible that all man's desire to make and establish comes. The simple structures of shelter seem like the markers of a dominating desire to establish a claim out of the vastness of the land, a place from which to dream of anticipated enterprise, full of the promise of a kingdom where the house or the castle is not yet in the mind.

Without historical records the story of America could come from the primitive desires and inspirations, the feeling of joy, which the endless unexplored land can evoke. The spirit of independence, our unique freedom, the feelings of unmeasured generosity and humble hospitality came from the spirit of the unrestricted spaces of the frontier.

The stone and wood, not bought but found, are used true to the rights one dares to take in gratitude for the gifts of nature. These noble and most ancient materials which in all ages inspired numerous and beautiful variations in the expressions of their orders here were used true to their nature with clarity and economy.

Later the Architect appears, admiring the work of the unschooled men, sensing in their work their integrity and psychological validity. They now stand in silence, yet stir the fairy tale and tell of life.

Louis I. Kahn

PIONEER TEXAS BUILDINGS

A Geometry Lesson

GEOMETRY

Early Texas
architecture
is a
geometry
lesson.

All things
have form.

Natural forms

Geometric forms

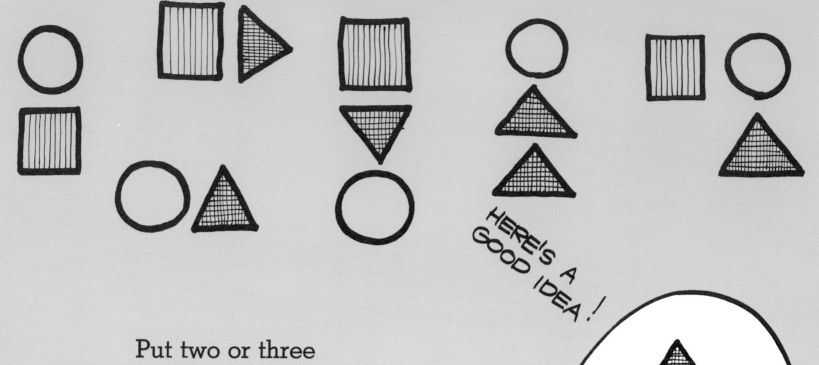

HERE'S A
GOOD IDEA!

Put two or three
simple geometric
forms together and
see what happens.

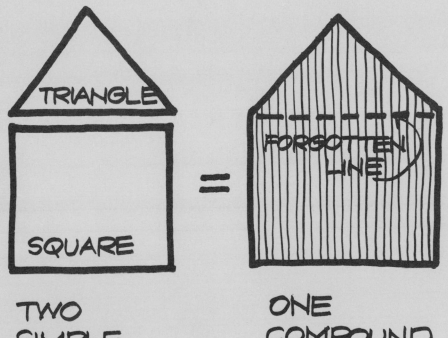

TRIANGLE

SQUARE

=

FORGOTTEN LINE

TWO SIMPLE FORMS = ONE COMPOUND FORM

Two forms put together make a compound form. The eye forgets the line in between. It reads the two forms together.

TRIANGLE &
SQUARE

½ TRIANGLE
& SQUARE

Put a house and
shed together.
See how it works.

COMPOUND FORM

Or add a barn and shed,

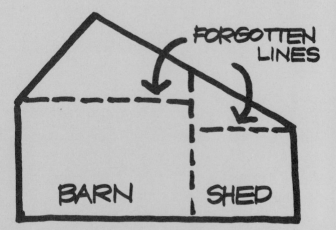

FORGOTTEN LINES

BARN | SHED

or add a barn and two sheds,

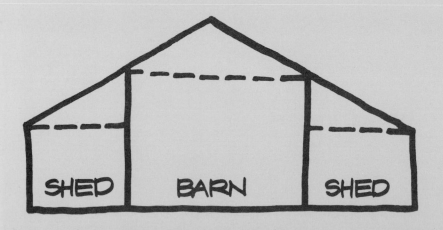

SHED   BARN   SHED

or **SUBTRACT** a porch from a house.

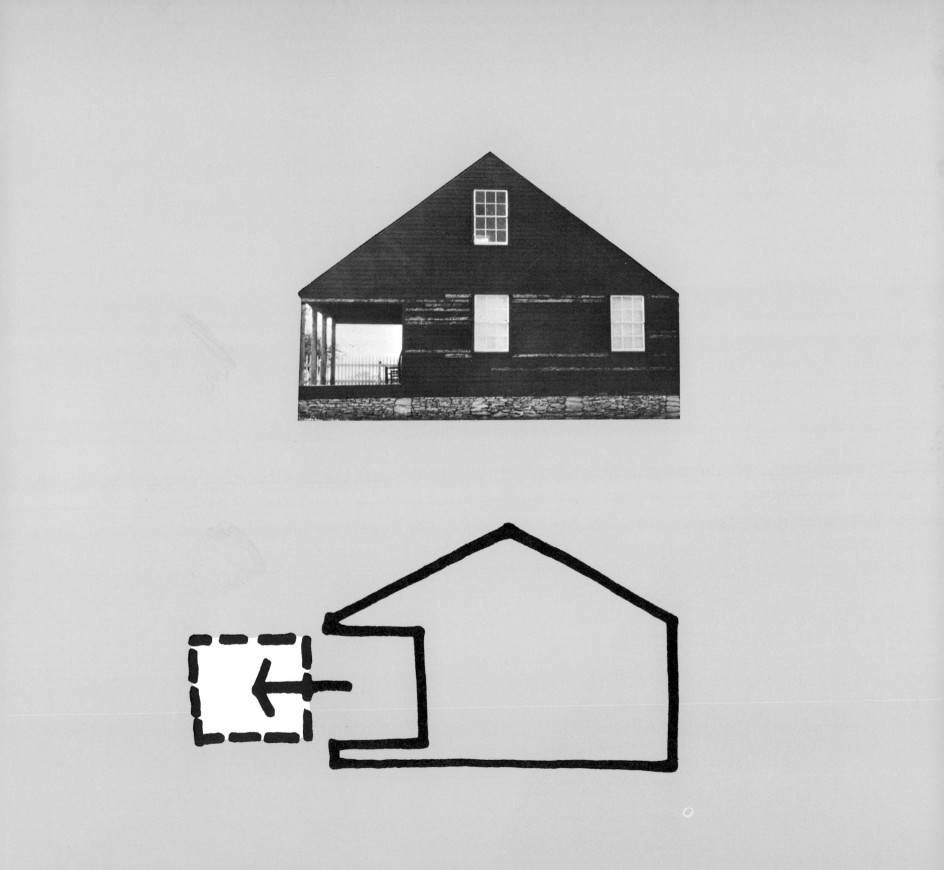

THINK
BIG!

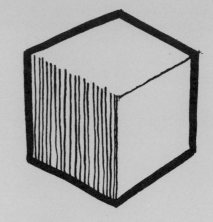

SQUARE → CUBE

Geometry is
three dimensional,
and so is
architecture.

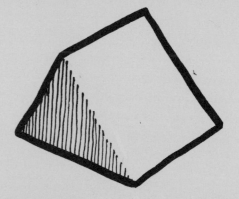

TRIANGLE → SOLID

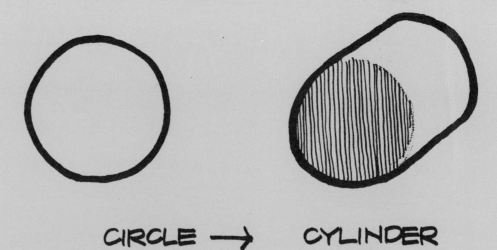

CIRCLE → CYLINDER

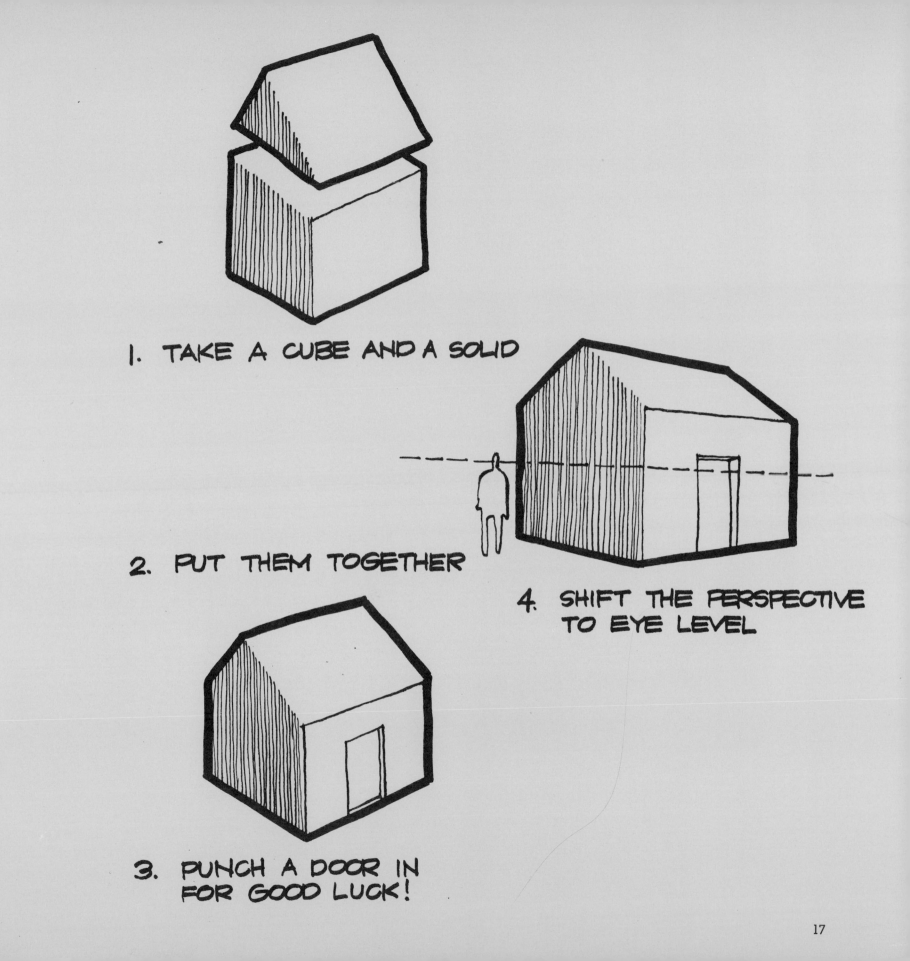

1. TAKE A CUBE AND A SOLID

2. PUT THEM TOGETHER

3. PUNCH A DOOR IN FOR GOOD LUCK!

4. SHIFT THE PERSPECTIVE TO EYE LEVEL

The "BASIC"

The building formed is the early Texas "basic." Things are added or subtracted but the friendly "basic" always remains—just a cube with a triangular solid on top.

The "basic" again.

The "basic" with a shed volume added.

All buildings are made up of solids and voids. The solid is the mass of the building, the void is the open part of the building. Windows and doors punched into the mass of a building are voids. An open porch, covered only by a roof but with no sides, is also a void. Early Texas buildings are composed first by simple geometries stacked together, second by solids and voids.

See how these ideas explain the house shown here.

The house is a "basic" with two sheds, one a solid, one a void. Punched in the solid are three additional voids, two windows and a door. With these ideas the house is completely defined.

Voids are two-dimensional (holes in a plane, such as windows and doors).

Voids are also three-dimensional (holes in the cubic volume of the building).

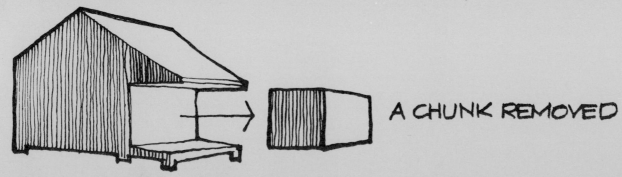

A CHUNK REMOVED

How did these forms get that way?

They needed to have this shape to get the job done. Early Texas houses, barns, and sheds are completely functional. Form follows function and nothing is left over.

All the parts have a job to do.

In this barn the "basic" is surrounded by sheds. In the barn on the right voids open into the center volume or into the sheds.

PORCHES

It is hot in Texas. The early Texas house has a porch of some kind. Porches are either integral, that is, part of the main volume, or added, with two volumes connected.

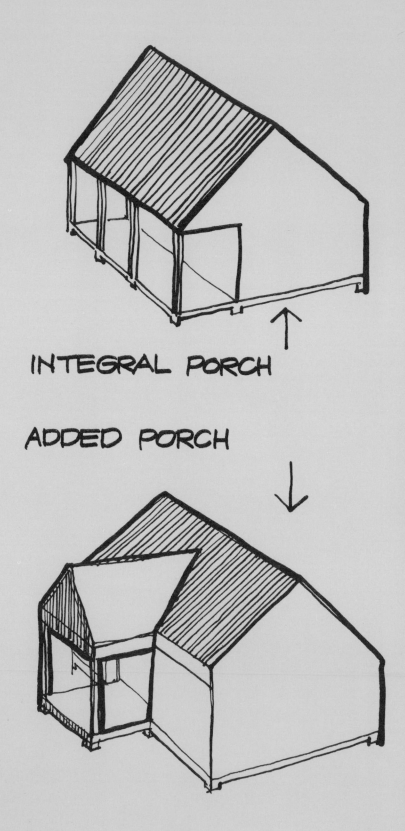

INTEGRAL PORCH

ADDED PORCH

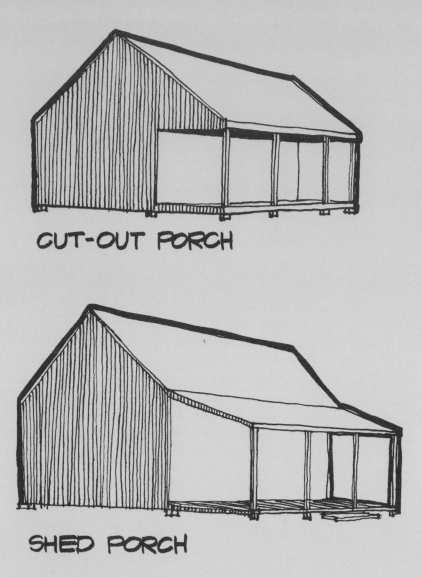

CUT-OUT PORCH

SHED PORCH

INTEGRAL PORCHES

POG-RUN PORCH

2-STORY PORCH

Two-story porches give second-floor rooms shade and views to both front and rear. They have much greater volume, and are more difficult to build than cut-out porches.

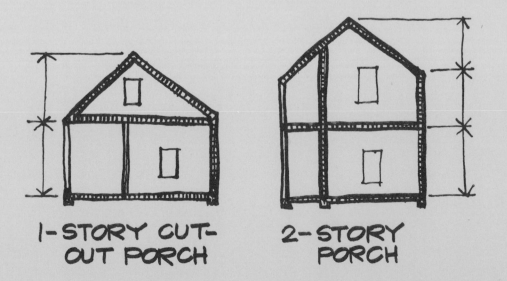

1-STORY CUT-OUT PORCH

2-STORY PORCH

Cut-out porch.

A cut-out porch has a low, low room above.

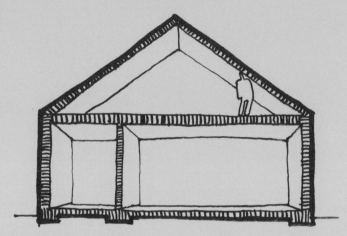

Push up the center section so that people can stand up.

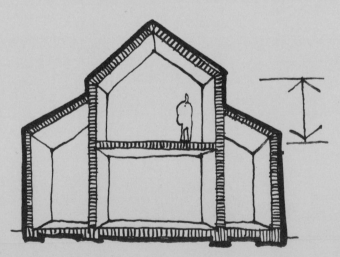

The cut-out porch becomes a shed porch.

More
shed
porches.

Another shed porch.

Shed roofs turn a corner.

Houses with porches in the middle are called dog-run houses. The breeze circulates through the house. In a sense it's two houses under one roof. When positioned to receive the prevailing winds the house is as cool as it can be on a Texas summer day.

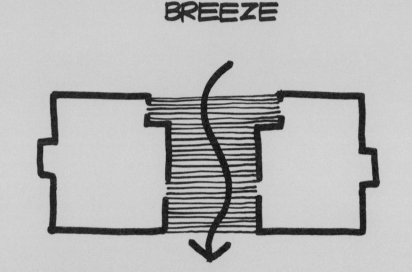

A two-story
dog-run
porch.

A two-story porch with an added porch surrounding the central building.

The two-story porch "classic."

A second-story porch
hung off the building.

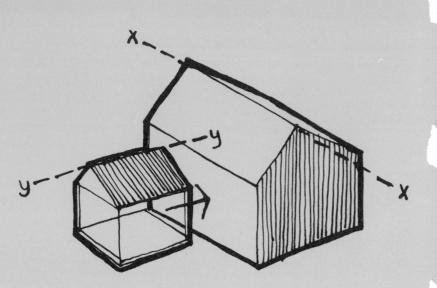

Two forms at right angles to each other are pushed together to make the cross-axis porch.

ADDED PORCHES

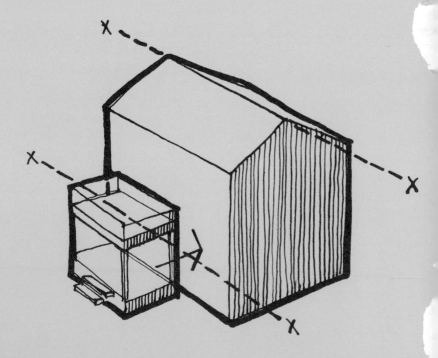

Two forms parallel to each other make a lateral porch.

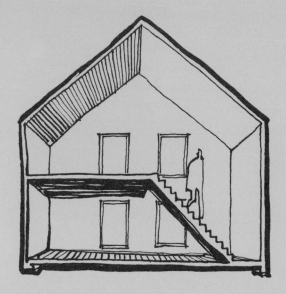

Most stairs are inside the house.

STAIRS (geometrically, an inclined plane).

They lead to the triangular volume above.

Some stairs are outside the house, either at the end of the Texas "basic" or within the porch. These stairs become part of early Texas geometry.

Outside stairs lead to a very low space above, used for storage or sleeping.

The main floor is half a level above the street; a basement is below.

This is an early Texas "split level."

Why does the early Texas house have outside stairs? They save valuable space inside and allow two families to use the same house. A covered porch stair provides some rain protection.

CHIMNEYS

Texas can be very cold. The chimney shape covers the "fire box" which is wide below and the flue which is narrow above.

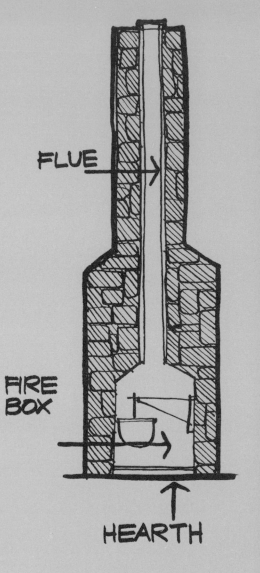

FLUE

FIRE BOX

HEARTH

All the form of a chimney and fireplace is functional.

Outside

Inside

STEEPLES

All the form in an early Texas church is functional, too, but in a different way.

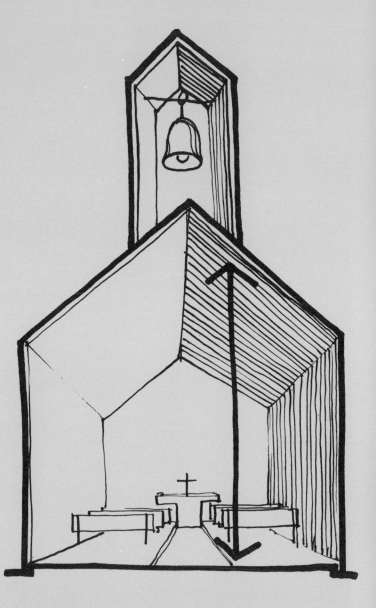

The Texas "basic" opens up full height inside. When a steeple is added, it holds the bell.

071405

77

Without a steeple the early Texas church is a simple
volumetric form.

Here the steeple is set on top of the basic form of the church and is secondary to it.

or the steeple is set at the
corner of the basic church.

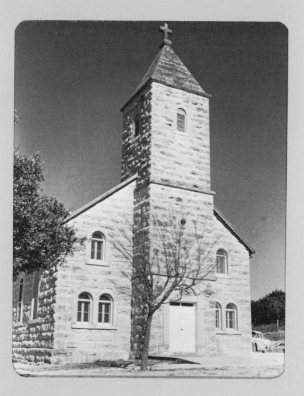

This steeple is placed in front
of the church form and is
therefore the major form.

MATERIALS

The early Texas builder had only simple materials to build shelter for family and animals.

Trees for wood.

Mud for stucco.

Rock for walls.

Most often the house or barn is built of wood.

Earliest buildings are
log structures.

Half-timber bracing is used to reinforce the walls.

Some buildings are built with solid stone walls which support the roof rafters above.

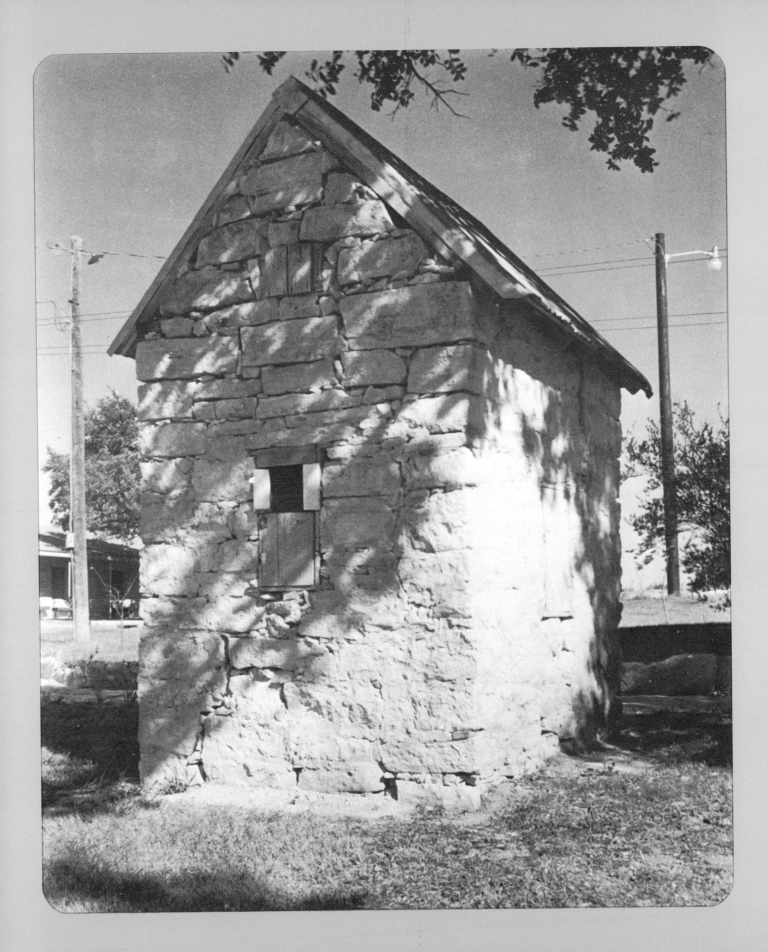

Board and batten siding, often of cedar or cypress, does not need paint to withstand the weather.

It's the form that really counts in architecture.
Decoration buzzes around the form to dress it up.

people in houses,

BARNS   The same shapes are used for

animals in barns.

Barns are simple geometries made up of solids and voids. The arch form is natural to masonry, for it carries the weight of the wall across the opening.

BUILDINGS

TOGETHER.

A house and barns make a farm.

Many houses make a town.

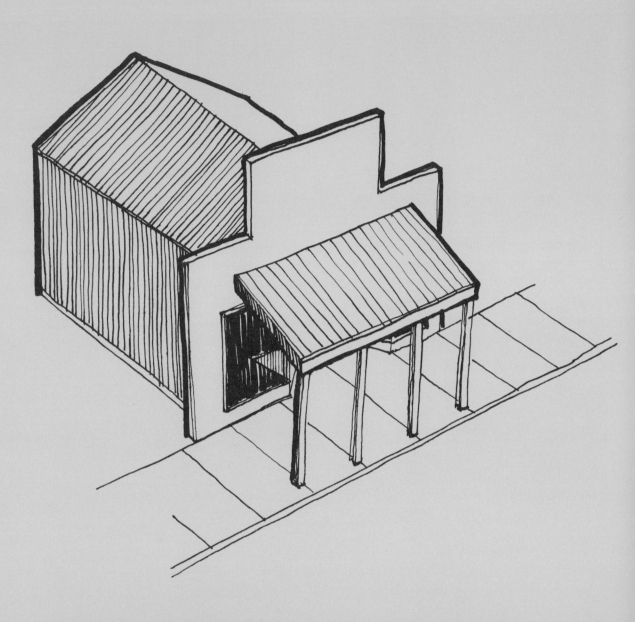

STORES
are in towns.

Rectangles face the street, sheds cover the entrance, and the glass opens up the inside. It is still a triangular roof on a rectangular base. Some stores have a false front to make them look bigger.

Many Texas stores are brick.

The brick arch is structural.

The decoration of the brick fronts gives them identity.

Where can these early
Texas buildings be found?

In Salado, Texas

On Route 36 near Caldwell, Texas

On Route 16 near Kerrville, Texas

In Round Top, Texas

On Route 16 between Fredericksburg and Kerrville, Texas

On Route 1457 near Round Top, Texas

Carmine, Texas

Honey Creek, Texas, on Route 46

Camp Verde, Texas

POSTSCRIPT

Early Texas buildings brought me back to Texas. A hundred times I drove down dusty roads through bleak countryside and discovered again a hundred different moods of homes or towns. A hundred moods sprang up from this remembrance and I had to come home. We can talk about the geometry of these early Texas buildings and that is their glory, but it is the poignancy of the environment they create, set in the Hill Country, that is the "why" of this book. It would be so easy to forget that, first and foremost, architecture is a reality; it must be dissected to understand how it is formed, so that it can be seen, so that we can learn to see. But the end, the reason, the adventure is the feeling of it; it is the mood it creates; it is the reality of responding to a man-made form, a man-made space.

Early Texas buildings brought me back to Texas. It took me five years to discover it. As this book grew, it became clear to me that these houses had been speaking to me since I had first known them as a child; they had been telling me something about simplicity, order, geometry, about how Texas was a hundred years ago. I have felt the need to say something about architecture; suddenly, in these houses, I found that it was about them I wanted to speak. This book lets it out; this book lets me go on; this book helps me see architecture in basic terms and I want it to speak to others. Architecture is a great adventure and when we see it, when we respond to it, we are richer.

I want these houses to speak out against the sham of current American domestic architecture. The fraud is so appalling, it becomes the aesthetic sin of the age by its very magnitude: that we snug Americans can live in our endless four-square rooms with our endless eight-foot-high ceilings while the outsides say everything stylistically under the sun is a fraud — we want it, so we have it. But it damages our spirit to acknowledge this fraud. Our eyes are dulled to the things of architecture, for they accept window trimming, the memory overlay of decoration, in place of significant form, significant space, or the synthesis of the two. A Polynesian broken-eave roof has the same stuffings inside as a French Provincial mansard-roof façade, or an Old English façade. We are building townhouses today with a Disneyland disregard for form; no one calls fraud when he sees fake plywood chimneys popped on top of gingerbread roof forms. No one calls fraud about a row of townhouses in alternate styles: one French, one Spanish, one Early American. At least we could have the aesthetic decency to admit that all the townhouses in France were French, in England, English, and in Spain, Spanish. With formal fraud on top of formal fraud no wonder we have so much trouble seeing architecture, no wonder our eyes are dimmed. And the fraud is institutionalized; each Sunday across the country a Home Building Section appears, calling these stylistic frauds beautiful, elegant, classic, and well balanced. A generation is growing up believing only the fraud, believing their parents live in a beautiful home because the paper says that a large, aluminum-windowed, two-carred, interior-bathed, vinyl-floored "Early Colonial" is beautiful.

Do we have a problem? We have a problem.

Let's try to see architecture again. Let's start out again; let's see if our eyes can lead our hearts to a new adventure. It doesn't have terms, it has no style, it is a way of seeing. In a world that wants to be "tuned in" and in an age that wants real experience, don't forget the glory, the reality of architecture.

A building is *space and form*. It is a strange and wonderful duality. It is the only form we experience both inside and out; not even in the cave do we really experience the duality, for we can conceive the space within but not the mountain. Outside, a building is an object which can be seen from a distance, small enough to put in our pocket. If we want to control a building visually, we need only walk away from it; sooner or later it's small enough for our ego and we can stop; we've mastered it. Come closer and we're in trouble; any building begins to grow up to overpower us, blank out the sky, and then all at once the moment of visual truth — we step through! No Alice in Wonderland looking glass was ever more exciting than this adventure we experience a thousand times a day. We pass through, space-to-space outside, then space-to-space from outside to inside . We're jaded or it would stop us; we're jaded or the wonder of it would haunt us; we're jaded or the two environments — the one outside we control, the one inside that controls us — would intrigue us. Not many years ago men felt this mystery of entering; throughout history man has made his entry point impressive, he has given it dignity. To look in or out was an act as worthy: the windows, the holes slashed in this form-giving skin, were gracious in size, decorated to entice the eye. Whatever the style, whatever the material, whatever

the age, man will move through space, man will continue the mystery of entering and leaving form. And he'll do it from a five-foot, two-inch-high eye level. He'll walk through space or drive, but the measure of man will be the same as it has been throughout history. Incredible, it's architecture.

There are really *four* things that architecture does. It creates *interior space* that envelopes us. It creates an *exterior object,* the formal husk of the space within. It creates *exterior spaces* by the grouping of objects in space (call them buildings if you must) which leaves a space in between. Finally, by superimposed buildings it creates *corporate forms* like the skyline of a city. With these simple things to do, architecture makes our environment. If thoughtfully done, if architecturally done, it enhances our mood. Our environment speaks to us, gives us something of our inner longing to be masters of our world, of our short life, of the incredible endless mystery. Without architecture, without thought, the forms still act on us, but the mood is fragmented, it builds nowhere, it becomes an environmental limbo, as most of our environs are today. Our junkyard of thoughtlessly formed cities and our sloppy countrysides are not wrong unless mediocrity is wrong; they are not evil unless it's evil to deprive man of art; they are not worth changing unless to know something of the power of form is important.

Thus, when you find simply stated geometric truths in houses, set quietly in the pensively rugged countryside of Texas, it is important. Architecture is space/form. It is a space within and an object without. When this inner form and outer form are one-one (the form expresses completely the space within) it's refreshing to say the least! In pioneer Texas buildings all the space is used: If the roof is a shed form the space inside is a shed form; if the roof outside is a pitch form the space inside is a pitched-ceiling space. Delightfully, the porches do all sorts of things: they are added forms, they are cut-out voids, they turn corners, they are dog-runs dividing the form in two parts — a thousand variations on the same theme, using interior spaces, exterior porches, and clear, related geometries.

Clusters of these forms make farms or towns. Many of the early towns are around a square, like Gonzales, Hallettsville, or New Braunfels. Sometimes the square is immense, as at Castroville, or minute, as at Round Top. Sometimes there is a sequence of squares, as in Anderson. It's not St. Mark's Square but it's real, it works on you just the same. Sometimes a town hall is dropped in the middle of the square, the space is lost, and the object of the pretentious town hall is so big that you wonder what they had in mind. For me, it's the ribbon of store fronts as in Comfort, Waelder, and Schulenburg that makes the statement for exterior space. These fronts become a wall, a line, often paralleling the train track with a ghost wall on the other side almost too far away to be felt. It's a ribbon space, a passing-through space, and it seems entirely appropriate to Texas, where going through takes more of your time than stopping. You are always going through town. It's the farm that is the cul-de-sac place to stop. In Texas, space is endless; you leave the passed-through town, end at the arrived-at farm. The most wonderful example of this is visiting Lange's Mill outside Fredericksburg. There is a special magic world behind that barn with the waterfall, the farmhouse, and the space across to the enclosing barns downhill.

We live by moods — a thousand times a day we feel them. Most don't stick and become a part of the fabric; when they do they become part of our person, our reality. I rather think in an afterlife we will remember them still — if so, would they not be religious? Such a mood I relate to this farm. I felt the mood there keenly and can recall it clearly as a precious remembrance.

Architecture is geometry/structure. All forms have form — sounds simple-minded but it leads somewhere. Forms must be sorted out and stacked in our minds in order for them to have meaning for us; rather, in order for us to understand our visual world through the symbol of these forms. Forms must be categorized for survival. Natural forms we can break out easily partly by what they are not. They are not geometric; geometry gives us mastery over forms, for we can conceive of them, use them, make building blocks out of them. As I write, I'm looking outside at the nongeometric, uncontrollable "formless" form of trees. The leaves shift, the light makes patches, the forms recede. Try as I might I cannot control them. Luckily, I have the view ordered by the geometric square of my window.

Buildings are basic geometries because it is through systems of mathematical order that we transcribe form, that we order our physical environment. To talk about an x-x axis and a y-y axis makes as much sense in the geometry of form as it does in the geometry of electromagnetic fields. Geometry is an ordered projection of our thought patterns; it expresses how we think about the concrete. Love isn't geometric, but science is.

But we have to build buildings that stand up — at least for a while. Geometry and structure become cosponsors of form when the building is unself-conscious and the relationship is one-one. Forms are added together in a simple geometry and they translate the loads to the ground. All the fine architectural forms we find in brick and stone buildings express this form-structure duality nicely, since a curve is the structural path of a load carried by small members in compression. They aren't the designed arches we pop onto our pseudo-Spanish façades to look round and pretty; they are structural arches that carry the load of the wall. Often, today, we don't need the arches to carry the load (for we have steel to span across lintels; we have wood walls behind the brick to carry the weight of the brick and roof to the ground). Why aren't we using the freedom today, opening the walls as never before? Why not go beyond a structural limitation and find a new reason for ripping through the enclosing skin?

Pioneer buildings in Central Texas are a geometry lesson. The forms are simply put together; there is a clear if uncomplicated structural integrity behind them (in the wood houses it is merely responding to the plainer quality of wood frame construction). These simple geometries are expressive of the space within in a simple one-one way. Yet the buildings relate to the special features of their sites, to settings almost as undisturbed as any in America. The environment is saying something to us, much as it did to men who lived simple lives a hundred years ago. In the book, I have stayed out of the cities, stayed apart from the Spanish influences, although these are important in Texas and carry a strong mood quotient. I have wanted to stay where the problem is a simple one, without a style overlay, without the encrustation of change brought on by time. It is in the predominately German towns of Central Texas where this kind of architecture says its simple piece over and over again.

How did it happen that we have this treasure? Texas history spells it out and these houses are there to affirm it.

There is a path running from the Gulf of Mexico to Dallas, with settlements dropped as cut-ants drop leaves along their way. It is in this area that houses are clustered. As inevitable as the geometry of architecture is the geometry of nature and man's response to it. He came from Europe, across a different substance than he could walk on, and so he used a boat — incidentally, it may be the other form we experience as an object and as a space, at least a boat in drydock where we can see all of it; rather exciting to think of a boat as a house covered almost halfway by water. A boat is a house on its side so the porch is on top and you must run down into the rooms. Or perhaps a house is a boat set on its side so you can run out. But the tyranny of physical geometry controlled our immigrant arrivals as much as the tyranny of that enclosing skin that separates the inside and outside of our houses. The best they could do was arrive in Texas by the Gulf. First arrivals were explorers, the historians of newness who left us their names for the mystical thing they did here: La Salle, arriving in Matagorda Bay in 1685, making it all right for German immigrants to come to the same bay in the 1840's, some 150 years later; Coronado, De Soto, now relegated to automobiles, were then giants in space, the astronauts of another age. I knew an astronaut very well, one that died; did I know La Salle a little bit, or Coronado, or the incredible Franciscan priests who set up shop on this moon of yesterday? Have I ever known the cruel, incredible Hernando Cortez, who tramped over the Aztecs in 1519, a hundred years before the explorers started. Who was Cortez?

Who were the Germans who landed in thousands in the 1840's? (I know them, for one of them was named Heimsath.) Whatever social, interpersonal tyrannies drove him from Germany—perhaps the dictator Metternich, perhaps the potato famines sweeping Europe in those years — he came and thousands more. He exchanged an interpersonal tyranny for a natural one. He arrived in Galveston, and then went to Indianola for a trek across Texas, to a land grant somewhere above Fredericksburg. In 1846 he saw his friends die of cholera. In any of the other years he fought Comanches, he heard of bandit raids, he lived with the interpersonal tyrannies of the New World on top of the droughts of Texas.

Before 1836 and Texas independence, Mexico promoted colonies. The most successful were led by Stephen F. Austin and Green C. DeWitt. In 1836 Texas armies defeated Santa Anna in some treacherous coastal plain geography, won independence, and intensified immigration. Read the story of the Adelsverein, a society of German princes set up to properly handle the German immigration and to protect their countrymen in the New World. It tells us why New Braunfels is where it is and Fredericksburg and many of the other German settlements from the Gulf northward. For sheer incompetency it was unparalleled; yet it got land deeded, it drummed up Texas in Germany, it inspired my forefathers to get out before things in Germany got worse. I would like to keep alive the historical fiction that Central Texas is all German. Actually, only a small proportion, say

20 per cent, of the immigrants came from Germany, but these came early and in organized lots and they settled their cities first. They helped establish the format of the cities, gave them their names, often German, as New Braunfels, Weimar, Frelsberg, New Ulm, Boerne. Polish settlers and already-Americanized settlers from the other states made up the vast part of the other newcomers. Fortunately, for Texas and for this latter-day look, the economy on the whole was not slave. There were few slaves in this central area, so studying pioneer homes has no problem of social guilt, something I wrestle with in affirming plantation architecture.

Life in Central Texas in the second half of the nineteenth century was isolated, rugged, simple, and hard. The houses reflect the virtue of this life. In our age, jaded by a plethora of forms, by visual stimuli screaming to be heard, it is an experience aesthetically and spiritually to follow again a dusty road, to find again the simple form of pioneer Texas houses. Perhaps at twilight is the best time — when a nightly form dismemberment takes place, if our eyes are tuned to see it and our minds can rejoice in discovering. The form of the object, expressing the space within, dissolves little by little into the nature that encompasses it, the nature that encompasses the house, the house that encompasses you — unless you must break through the skin of enclosing form and sit outside on the defined exterior space of the porch, unless you feel the anxiety of the quiet upon you and you must leave the house entirely and stand under the form of the sky, surrounded only by the now no longer amorphous form that is the mountains, and wonder about the stars.

Clovis Heimsath

ILLUSTRATIONS

Map courtesy, Humble Oil & Refining Company, ©General Drafting Co., Inc.

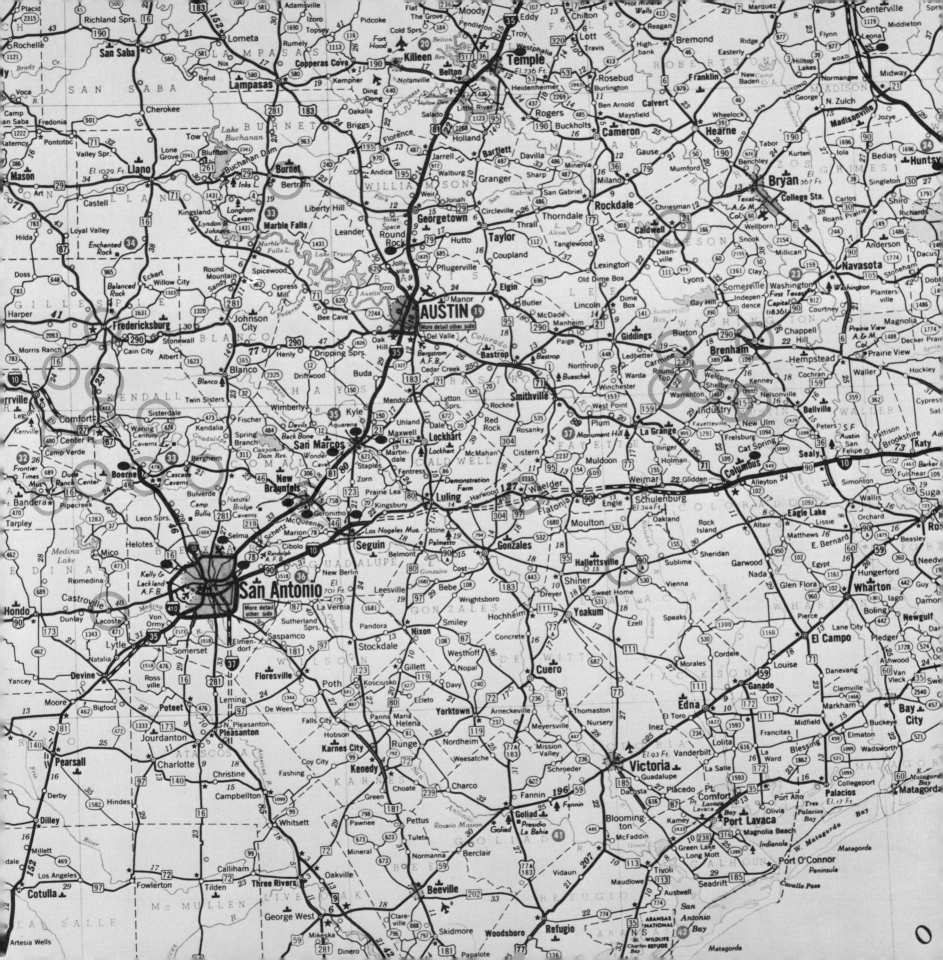